a Peace of my Mind

~Inspiration~

To Ms. Brenda Carter:
Thanks so much for showing me kindness. You are specially made. God has great things for you, so stay focused & stay encouraged!

Poetry that will touch your soul...

by f. shepbyrd

Lantia
3/2001

a Peace of my Mind: Life & Love / Inspiration

Book/Cover Design and Layout by F. Shepbyrd

For more information, questions or comments about these and/or the full collection of poems, or ordering, please contact:

Rhythm & Rhyme Publishing
PO Box 444
Antioch, TN 37011-0444
(615) 731-5642

ISBN: 0-9704928-1-2

Library of Congress Control Number: 00-092644

First Printing
Printed in the United States

Acknowledgements

A Peace of my Mind is peace in my heart. I first thank God for giving me a gift that helps me to heal. I thank God for giving me a gift I can share.

I am inspired to write as a way to express my thoughts, feelings and experiences from everyday life. I hope something I'm expressing in this select group of poems encourages you, somehow, in what you may feel and/or need to express.

Last, but not least, I truly thank my family at Greater Emmanuel In Faith Ministries in Nashville, who have helped guide and support me in my faith walk. Also, to every other child of God who has ever shared words of encouragement or given the support needed to help get me through some of the situations reflected in my poetry, I truly, truly appreciate every word, every prayer (family, friends, preachers, teachers, mentors, and yes, singers, too). Thank you.

"...Inspiration" is dedicated to all who love the Lord and
want to follow His ways....
and to those who have yet to seek Him.
Just remember to...

Hold On

When you're beaten down by your past
And feeling you won't last, hold on.
When it all seems so hopeless
And "it" just doesn't make sense, hold on.
When you're discouraged, though you try
Yet, constantly look to your last dime, hold on.
When you're in the deepest pain
From the problems that often reign, hold on.
When you're in despair
And feeling too weary to care, hold on.
When you just want to die
Because you can no longer cry, hold on.
When you're feeling lonely...
To the Lord's hands, only...
hold on.

over hills and mountains

The grassy field You made for me
Is just a step toward eternity
The rainy day that restores from drought
Is You showing there's no need to doubt
Bright sunny days nearly blinding eyes
Is a way You smile away demise
A desert of sand, dry and burning
Is wanting to know You with such a yearning
We see valleys, big cities, forests with trees
Things You've made, to us, with ease
Blessings all over, each and every day
For those who love You and want to follow Your ways
We climb step by step, may stumble and fall
Yet, You're always right there to help endure it all
Through the hills and mountains and unreachable peaks
Your love and promises are our strength when we're weak
No matter the weather or highest of mounds
You're the answer to overcoming with leaps and bounds
Over the hills and mountains, whatever we go through
Each effort is just another step closer to You.

I'm Rich

inspired by Minister Gregory Roberson

You think I'm rich because of money?
Oh, honey,
let me
tell you of He
He who is rich
and provides me with
everything I need,
indeed,
see, if you love Him
He lives within
then, your pot of gold
will be found in your soul
see, my Father is rich
and, He provides me with
everything I need,
indeed,
and, for the things I want
it's faith that is taught
for God knows my heart
and, from Him, I won't part
so, you see, it's because of He,
He who blesses me
that I can live as if
I am one who is rich.

I prayed for you

to all who've filled my heart

Last night, I prayed for you
and asked the Lord to lift you up
Last night, I prayed He'd help you
in the places you feel stuck
I asked Him to send you His grace
and keep you in His arms
And asked Him to let you know He's there for you
in the midst of your storms
Then, this morning, I prayed for you
and thanked God for a new day
I thanked him for letting you rise, like me,
and for letting you know His ways
I thanked Him for your presence in my life
and the joy you've brought to me
I thanked Him for sharing with me
the blessing of harmony
As I travel the paths of each new day,
you remain in my heart
I ask the Lord to work through us
as we keep Him the center part
I wonder sometimes what He has for us
as we struggle to do what's right
But, all in all, I know He loves us
for we still look up high

Each night as I still pray for you,
know that you are dear
And every morning, when I open my eyes,
I ask God to keep you near.

Thou Shalt Not Covet

What you have, I may not have,
but that doesn't make you better than me.
What I get, you may not get,
but that's only because He says it's for me.
Jealousy, envy – not ways of the Lord
but salvation is what you'll find on the other side of His door
My gifts are mine, you have yours, too,
He does no less that what He says He'll do.
Each of us unique – particular to what we receive
The only thing you can have like mine is His love and liberty.

Untitled

In Jesus' name,

I can make that claim

of all that's possible

because, He says, it is so...

In Jesus' name.

Listen to the Quiet

Listen to that quiet whisper
the voice is calm and still
you know that no one was in your ear
yet the voice just seemed so near
the words are sure
the voice is pure
if you follow and listen close
you'll find the message is loud and clear
from the one you should trust the most.

Pass It On

Pass it on...
love
encouragement
compassion
a listening ear.

Pass it on...
joy
inspiration
comfort
a praying heart.

Pass it on...
sincerity
endearment
confidence
kindness in Spirit.

Pass it on.

My Shield

Your mighty ways
You show me each day
as I see the daylight
and listen for ways right
each gentle breeze
You wrap around me
like the arms of one strong
who would shield me from harm
I cling to You
for I know You are true
loving and enduring
through whatever life brings
You show me the way to go
by myself, I wouldn't know
but I feel you near
instead of giving in to fear
which is not of You
because You are the one who
takes care of me.

Encircle Me

for Amber, Derrick and Rod

Lord, please encircle me with Your angels,
Encircle me with Your grace
Encircle me so I can conquer the adversity I may face
Encircle me with Your love and peace,
Encircle me with Your power so each
  vision You show me I can reach
Encircle me, please, Lord, encircle me.

Fight

for dad

Put on the whole armor
and prepare to fight
with all of your might
despite
what's not in sight
but is right
and due
to you
just do
according to
God's truth
for the good
you produce
as you review
life, subdue
strife,
avoid pride
don't fear the night
but be kind and,
keep Christ in mind
and, you will find
He's always right on time.

New Direction

for Richard

I can't move my feet
until You show me how to walk
I can't make my speech
until You tell me how to talk
A better direction
that's what's truly sought
On my own,
I've always struggled and fought
If You lead me
I can embark on more
If I follow You
You'll point me to open doors
My way is vague
I don't know what to do
Confusion settles in
until I truly seek You
I need a new direction
for the life You've given me
If I follow Your instructions
I can be as great as You want me to be.

Believe in Me

Believe in Me
I will make you free
the choice is yours
if you want My Spirit poured
on you
what you must do

is claim My name
this is not a game
I am for real
My salvation does heal
a love so true
I died for you

so your life could be
lived in liberty
don't look away
this is the day
just call on Me
I will always be

the Son of the Father
who wants to be bothered
with you

but what you must do
is let Me in
I'll cleanse you from sin

I will love you so
just don't let Me go
I'll be here for you
I am the truth
your life will be rich
for, I've provided you with

My Holy Word
many will be heard
who speak in my name
My spirit can't be tamed
get to know Me
then you will see

with Me, you'll achieve
but, first, you must believe
love, obey and trust
in me, your friend, Jesus.

Wonderful

Wonderful Maker
Soul Shaker
Sin Taker
How great you are
To have gone so far
To create the stars
The planets, sun and moon
which wasn't too soon
And, a Heaven with plenty of room
How Wonderful to see
How great you'd still be
To save a lost soul like me.

Love is

inspired by and dedicated to my friends in Voices of the Heart

Love is
the sun rising and the sun setting each day

Love is
the vision of a colorful sky as the gift of a
rainbow forms through the clouds

Love is
a warm smile from friendly faces and
humble souls

Love is
a bit of cheer when a heart is broken
with sadness

Love is
the hand of God that always reaches for us
when we reach for Him.

My Angel On Earth

He knew I needed what I could not see
He sent me that blessing when He sent you to me.
You were my gift from the Heavens above
A very special way He sent me His love.
He couldn't come down Himself, no, not from there.
So, he sent me an Angel to show me He cared.

"A true saint," we'd say, serious about his job
Anointed and called to show the love of God.
What you brought to me, I couldn't repay.
Just having you near made, for me, great days.
My darling Angel, I've loved you so...
But now, back to God, I must let you go.

My Time !

You see my face
and you think it's a waste
for me to still grieve
cause time should have healed.

But you can't be aware
of the love that was shared
with this person who my life
was spent loving 'till he (or she) died.

A part of me has gone
so allow me my time to mourn
until my heart is freed
and the grief has been relieved.

This pain is only mine.
Please, let me have my time.

It ain't always what it seems...

However difficult our circumstances may be,
realize, it ain't always what it seems.
Remember when you asked for help with rent,
but money didn't come in time...
Or, you asked to get that promotion
but, instead, lost your job...
But, it ain't always what it seems.

You're troubled by your children's attitudes,
and, even after prayer, it seems to just get worse...
You asked to be healed of an infirmity,
yet, find yourself still unwell...
But, it ain't always what it seems.

God hears you.
He says, "My ways are not your ways, and my thoughts are not your thoughts..."
This is true.
Believe God knows best, even when He seems to have forgotten you
His plan for our lives rely heavily on our trust
Even though He seems absent, keep your faith throughout the disgust.

God has a way of making any bad good
and bringing understanding to what was misunderstood
He'll make our wrongs right
As long as we don't give up our fight
'Cause it takes seeing past the hard times to see the final product
He has in mind.
So, no matter how bad things may happen to be...
Remember, with God, it ain't always what it seems.

The Road

I left what I thought was my safety zone
to travel to another place.
I chose a way unfamiliar,
to change to a different pace.
This way was strange, I don't know why...
maybe because I didn't plan it.
I allowed myself to be led, this time,
to a road I've taken for granted.
Led by a Light, so bright and calm,
it took me toward great things.
I couldn't have found it myself, though I've tried,
for this was the way of the King.
Mighty but strong, a love so fierce,
following the Light leads no one wrong.
What a difference it is to know this road
is a sinner's way to the throne.

my 'vice (2U)

The life of a loser is one who quits much too soon
Don't you know about the kingdom, the one with plenty of room?
Dem vices holding you tight, refusing to ever let go
You can rely on the weapon, that of the Sovereign Hero.

Your baby's cryin', no food to eat
Pain with each wail that screams defeat
That man's runnin' round, lust he can't resist
The comfort of the bottled quiet so you can cease to exist
Your woman says she's leaving 'cause the money ain't quite right
She'd know a good thing if she'd just receive the Light.

Black eye, broken arm, lowered self-esteem
For this you said "I do," thinking this was your fairy tale dream.
Children waitin' for a mama who keeps answering that call to the streets
Tryin' to hold on to the youthfulness of an age she'll never again see.

Can't climb out of the hole the world's vices helped lead you in.
Unless you grab the rope the Saviour holds by the other end
The darkness is not the night when its all you seem to see
But, Salvation, glory and peace is there waiting to set you free
Be strong enough to give in to God, let go of the stronghold
My 'vice 2 U is to let Him show you the way to those streets of gold.

Set It Free

Set it free
Whatever it may be
That has you tied and bound
So your blessings can come around.

Give it up
That part of your life that's corrupt
Peace is near
If your heart is sincere.

Let it go
Our Father in Heaven knows
He will take it from you
If your faith in Him is true.

Set it free
It was released on Calvary
We are not to be bound
Our salvation was long ago found.

I Pray

Lift me up, Oh Lord
that I might know your ways
Lift me up, Oh Lord
where, in me, Your Word remains
Lift me up, Oh Lord
that I might do Your will
Lift me up, Oh Lord
in me, Your spirit instilled
Lift me up, Oh Lord
that I may follow Your lead
Lift me up, Oh Lord
that I may help the blind see.

Your Love

I know you love me
Because You let me stand yet
Though I meet much adversity
It is me, Lord, You never forget

I know you do love me
You've kept Your hand over my life
Through all the heartaches and pain
It's been You whose led me out of the strife

I know how much You do love me, Lord
You answer each time I call
I want to one day see Your face
I wish Your love could reach all.

Where Are You Going?

Where are you going,
and what's your plan?
Are you like a gypsy
traveling the land?
Have you found your dreams
fading like footprints in washed-over sand,
Or do you seek direction from the great I AM.

Where are your going,
and what's your plan?
Do you rely on yourself,
or is it God's way you want to understand?
Do you seek guidance from the ungodly,
or have you sought the pointing finger of God's hand?
Who's planning the route of travel to get you to
your promised land?

Where are you going...
and where are you getting your plan?

Last Chance

something we all should think about...

If you had one last chance to change your life
Would you choose to do what's right?
If you were told this is the end,
Would you make the right choice on which your life depends?
If you know how you've struggled to do things on your own,
Would you choose to remain on this earth alone?
If you were told this is your last day to say goodbye
Would you choose eternal life or would you just prefer to die?

Time and time again, we are given a chance
To trust in a Master in whom we can take a stance
The choices we make are of our own will,
But, with God on our sides, He'll carry us over those hills.
If we could choose how to treat one another,
Would our neighbor be our enemy, or would we
love him like a brother?
If you had one last chance to change your evil ways,
Would you become an honorable person, or still wear a double face?
If you had one last chance to live your life unselfishly,
Would you share the goodness of your blessings, or still feel
'it's all about me.'

Think about having one last chance to change,
If you are broken, He'll take away your pain.
If you constantly suffer from doubt and worry,
Trust in the Lord, He'll answer soon, if not in a hurry
Everyone has had something that's been a battle and a trial,
But, only the true believers recognize the miracles of Christ in His
graceful style

He'll take the extremes and turn them around,
He'll loosen the ties that have had you bound,
His awesomeness is overflowing and is enough for each one who hears,
And, though we can't see Him, the trusting heart knows He is near.
If you had one last chance to make that wrong right,
Are you going to choose eternal death,
or do you want the abundant life?

So, what's on your mind?

Use the space below to write your own inspirational poem.

About the Author

Born and raised in Brooklyn, New York, F. Shepbyrd has had a love for the written word since her pre-school years. At age 12, she began to express her emotions and concerns in the form of poetry and short stories. Yet, it has taken several more years and various life experiences for her to recognize and appreciate that sharing her work through this special gift can positively touch the lives of others.

After completing a short term in active duty Air Force, F. Shepbyrd relocated to Nashville, Tennessee. She attended Nashville State Technical Institute, where she majored in Visual Communications/Graphic Design. She later transferred to Tennessee State University and has received a B.A. in English/Professional Writing.

She has been published in two anthologies of poetry, one of which is the International Library of Poetry's 2000 Anthology, *Nature's Echoes*. In addition, the semi-finalist poem *"If I Could Just Touch You"* has also been requested to be included on their special audio recording, "*The Sound of Poetry.*" Poems *"Untitled (A woman of...),"* and "*Beauty, the Beast*" were published in Tennessee State University's 1996 and 1997 *Literary Review*. As a part of *Voices of the Heart*, the local Christian poets' group she co-founded in 1999, she can be found reading some of her poems at various programs and events, as well as reading on her own at local Nashville coffee houses, such as Kijiji's Coffee House.

F. Shepbyrd has future plans to publish and promote other poets through her company, Rhythm & Rhyme Publishing, with hopes of bringing more light to the voice of poetry that is personal, as well as that which is inspirational to the reader. She continues to reside in the Nashville, Tennessee area and is currently developing a play based upon the various life challenges of which her poetry speaks about. Much of that poetry will also be incorporated into the script as dialogue.

a Peace of my Mind

~Life and Love~

Poetry that will touch your soul...

by f. shepbyrd

a Peace of my Mind: Life & Love / Inspiration

Book/Cover Design and Layout by F. Shepbyrd

For more information, questions or comments about these and/or the full collection of poems, or ordering, please contact:

Rhythm & Rhyme Publishing
PO Box 444
Antioch, TN 37011-0444
(615) 731-5642

ISBN: 0-9704928-1-2

Library of Congress Control Number: 00-092644

First Printing
Printed in the United States

Acknowledgements

A Peace of my Mind is peace in my heart. I first thank God for giving me a gift that helps me to heal. I thank God for giving me a gift I can share.

I am inspired to write as a way to express my thoughts, feelings and experiences from everyday life. I hope something I'm expressing in this select group of poems encourages you, somehow, in what you may feel and/or need to express.

Last, but not least, there are so, so many people I owe my thanks to. To each member of my e n o r m o u s family (especially on the Shepard, Byrd, Watson and Latimore sides), each friend (whether for a moment, a season, or for life), every one who has thought enough of my work to show support and encourage me to share my gift -- but especially my mother, who was the first to recognize it, and my father, both from whom I inherited this gift, I thank you.

"...Life and Love" is dedicated to
anyone who's ever loved ...
and lost...
and loved again.

And, also to you...you know who you are...

Many of these words belong to you... and me....

Now it seems like we've come to the end of this road...

Only God knows the rest...

But, thanks for giving me so much to write about...

I hope love reaches you one day...

And you finally reach back...

If I Could Just Touch You

If I could just touch you
I'd reach out, right to your heart
If I could just touch you
I'd reach deep down into your soul
If I could just touch you
I'd soothe those hurt feelings
If I could just touch you
I'd cuddle and hold you in the warmth of your spirit
If I could just touch you...
If you'd just let me get close to you
I'd show you the love of God...
If I could just touch you.

Untitled

A woman of substance: that's who I am.
Although, when you first met me, you thought I was just another,
Until you heard me speak words of character.
You wanted to look past me because of my ordinary appearance,
Until you saw that I, too, could capture your gaze – when I want to be seen.
You thought I carried little value -
    mistaking my tolerance for weakness
        my strength for dominance
            my wisdom for chatter.
But, I am a woman of substance.

You met me expecting to find what you had ordinarily come to know.
You envisioned me having just common attitudes
    with no foundation,
        basic traits lacking appealing uniqueness–
            a simple compound of little diversity.
Instead, you found in me what you've probably failed to find,
    yet may still hope for.
I offer you comfort, so your hardships are not your own,
    appreciation for the uniqueness of your qualities,
        affection for all the fineness you truly possess,
            support in all you need....
                when you need....
                    how you need...

So, whenever you see me standing in the background, remember:
I look as I do, because I am a woman of substance,
without needing to be flamboyant.
I act as I do, because I am a woman of substance,
who needs not to be strident.
I am the kind of woman our mothers of greatness
want their daughters to be.
I am the kind of woman who you,
my strong, Black brother, need.

If I

If I let you enter my world
will you take care of me?
If I let you enter that special place
will my heart remain free?
If I let you touch my soul
will you let me touch yours, too?
If I let your hands speak warmth to me
will love reach out from you?
If I let you into my deepest dreams
will you stay for the final scene?
If I let you wander away sometimes
will you return to me?
If I let you see the love inside of me
will you want to keep me close?
If I let you feel my fire and heat
will you desire me most?
If I let you know how special you are
will you do what you proclaim?
If I let you receive what you need from me
will I be blessed with the same?

What I Want

I want a man to love me
mind
body and
soul.

I want him to want to
grow with me
excel with me
achieve with me and
believe with me.

I want him to feel I'm
his everything
his dream come true and
his gift from God.

I want a man who
wants me to have
all of him . . .
Because he wants
all of me.

But, I don't just want a man.

Black Pride

My Beautiful Black man, my strong brother
He's one unlike any other
Through years of struggle and misbelief
He remains strong enough to achieve.

Put here to excel
Society has served him hell
Brown sugar queen mothers raised him to be bold
Through all hardships, for his children he is a mold.

A woman, a friend, a lover is she
He takes a strong woman--one as strong as he
Life's long path, they travel as one
He holds on to his woman--God's will be done.

He has beautiful tan skin or maybe dark brown
His woman of equal helps bring him around
Times will get rough, and he may be down
But both together can help keep him off the ground.

Joint efforts, dual roles, togetherness, success;
individuality, perseverance, past lives put to rest
Let him be himself, love him as he is
Let him be as great as he allows this woman of his.

To love a Black man is to love his human side
For many years, his wisdom they'd hide
His existence is a gift to all
His peers and loved ones tried to be there when he'd fall.

To the ladies:
To be a success doesn't mean no distress
Ladies don't desert him when he's doing his best
If he should fail, don't feel he's a failure
When his luck runs bad, stay with him in prayer
Give him what you've got; your love in all its ways.

To the fellas:
If she wants to comfort you, don't push her away
Keep the pride and machism to a minimum, it's more hurtful today
When you feel you're being wronged and it seems you're all alone
Look to your side, 'cause holding your hand is that woman you love.

People: Stop playing these childish games
Life is too short not to live in harmony...
Brothers and sisters, husbands and wives, parents and children,
Neighbors, lovers...
We have to stop fighting each other.

the family poem

dedicated to the Shepard Family 1999

we laugh, we cry
we help one another to survive
there's joy, there's pain
there's a love that always remains
there's the new, there's the old
a wonderful history time unfolds
we say hello, we say goodbye
holding on to our memories until next time...

That's what family's about.

New Generations

The first half of this poem is the quote of a fictional elderly neighborhood person who still has hope for a generation that is seemingly lost...

"I seen some chil'len just the other day...
'Dem chil'len can really be somebody in each of their own way.
Dat lil' boy there always playin' 'round in that dirt...
Wanna some day build skyscrapers all over the earth.
Ms. Mary's lil' girl still playin' with 'dem doll babies...
Think she soon be teaching some of our brightest young men and ladies.
'Dat boy over there always watching for emergency sites...
Said he wanna grow up to help keep people out of danger and save lives.
My great-grandbabies even have some great dreams.
I keep them encouraged, and hopeful, no matter how bad things seem.
One of 'dem chil'ren sure ain't bothered by no blood...
He say he wanna fix people and care for them with love.
And, my other great-grandbaby sure love to write...
She's touches other peoples' hearts, no maybe or might."

So many of our children are living in poverty
They need to know that's not how it always has to be
A dream is only worthwhile if we dare to make it come true
And, we need to let them know there isn't anything they can't do
There's a God above who looks out for all of our little ones
We must teach our children that they are God's daughters and sons
The world is round and can make for us a lifelong trip
If we have our dreams, make some goals, and be positive in how we live
Each child we see should be a future dream to come true
For they are the ones who will follow us as these generations continue.

A Mother's Love

to those who don't see it's a blessing just to have been born...
and given a chance...

She nurtured me in the warmth of her love
She was my first gift from God's heavens above
Keeping me in that special place inside
Loving me enough so I could survive
Two faces anxious to see one another
The close knit bond of a child and a mother
I could never repay her for taking care of me
Too many mothers, their child, never see
We didn't have to be here, but it was God's will
To allow chance after chance to be around still
People stay angry – souls house hurt
Feeling tossed away, as if no better than dirt
She cared enough to keep you within
A chance to live other than your origin
The gift of your life is precious to the Father
Forgive and love her because she did bother
To nurture and keep you as close as you could be
To offer you the chance to be as great as your destiny.

Who You Are

to A.J. & the other young brothers who represent greatness – yet, don't know it

Who are you? Don't you know?
You represent the future for the young men coming up after you.
You show the elders that their raising you has a value.
You are the threat to the society who thinks you are less.
You are an example that you're capable of being amongst the best.
So, why do you look and act like you don't know who you are?

An attitude that says you don't care.
An appearance that seems to show you won't dare.
Don't you know you're better than that?
Your desires should go beyond the societal stats.

So clean up your act,
Pull up your pants,
Take off that hat,
And don't say you can't...
or won't.

Your little brothers are looking up to you...
And, so are the little ladies who will someday want to love them.
Be proud.
Be bold.
Be positive.
Be an example.

My Greatest Inspiration

for my mom

A spirit so high
Your presence brings forth smiles

A love so deep
You're a friend well worth the keep

Your laughter, so full of joy
You are someone I truly adore

Your beauty radiates from the heavens to your heart
You've been faithful to those you care for from the start

There aren't enough people in the world like you
No gift or honor could surpass what you're due

When God smiles on and because of you, that's my confirmation
And the reason why you're my greatest inspiration.

Dream

my dream is of
peace
tranquility
love
joy
and
kindness.

it's about romance
passion
warmth
comfort
and
desire.

a guiding hand
a holding hand
a loving hand
a praying hand

and my dream
is
only
of
you.

Another Day

daylight came
but nothing changed
fantasies, dreams
real life, it seemed
thoughts of you
my mind reviewed
wanting the touch
that meant so much

kind words
never before heard
wondrous gestures
time is the tester
morals fight feelings
heartache again stealing
waiting around
for someone who's bound
time passes by
between each cry

you look...

you look like
somebody's brother
somebody's friend
somebody's father
somebody's "10"
somebody's lover
somebody's tank
someone's warm cover
someone's cold drink.
Shoot, you just look like
chocolate ice cream with hot fudge
piled high in a dish
I would take all day to savor you
Hmm...I only wish.

(to be continued)

Untitled

to those who "used to be"

Ouch! There's a pain in my back...

And, it's sharp and throbbing.

Can you look and see if anything's there?

What? I'm bleeding?!

No...No, I didn't fall.

No...I don't recall scratching too hard...

But, there are some scars from before.

God, it's sure hurts!

But, it will heal.

Hey, you know what?

What I do remember is

when you

stabbed me

in the back.

Silent Tears

I'm crying out
but you don't hear me
I'm needing you
but you don't feel me
I'm falling apart
but you don't see me
Please, just hold me
before you lose me.

be my man?

you cannot be my man
'cause you don't even know who I am
I don't need no fans
tryin' to be my man.

when you take the time to know me
you'll learn there's no greater possibility
I am everything you want and need
if you'd just see the value of you and me.

but, you can't be my man
and take my hand
until you know who I really am.

World of Sin

What is it about this world of sin
I'm living in
that keeps drawing me in
deeper and deeper
toward my own lusts
which I don't even trust
but feel I must
give in
to the sin
that draws me in
but I can't defend
this sin that must end
but won't ever bend
'cause it looks just like a friend
just stopping by again
maybe this time a different flavor
wanting me to savor
not to be put in a container
away from me
where I could be free
to resist the world of sin
that still seeks to draw me in.

You Owe Me

You don't owe me anything???
Oh, I think you do...
For what I've given you???

I've lifted you up when the ones you thought more of
kept their foot on you.
I gave to you, from my heart,
when you had nothing much to carry it all in.
I believed in you when you were so frustrated,
you almost stopped believing in yourself.
I gave of myself what I was saving for
that special someone, because I love you like that.
I gave you good conversation when others
just wanted to see that which was worth talking about.
I gave you appreciation for being the person you rarely
felt comfortable enough to reveal to others.
I gave you enough love to begin the rest of your life with--
the kind that was so good, it scared you.
I gave you a good friend, one who never judged you
or thought you had little value as a person.

So, yeah, you'd better believe you owe me...
You owe me respect, appreciation & consideration...
The same you would expect,
if it were you,
who had given to me.

Trail of Tears

Follow me through my trail of tears,
So you can understand the nature of my fears.
If you hold my hand and walk by my side,
You'd understand times I've struggled to survive.
When you take the time to see me through my days,
Then, will you understand the ways I've changed.
If you get soaking wet in the midst of my storms,
You'd find out how God makes me strong.
Follow me through my trail of tears,
It will make your heart for me sincere.

Golden Ribbons

I shadowed you with comfort
I covered you with care
I poured out golden ribbons
that came from my heart
and spread them all over
you
And you came back
with a vengeance
trying to make me reap what you had sowed
Planted honey-vinaigrette kisses
on these sugar-filled lips
that waited for you
What were you really saying
with those intense eyes
that looked like they were eating my
every
morsel
smiling that sexy smile
that used to melt me into the smooth
chocolate
that makes you so fine in my eyes
the eyes
that wanted to cover you

with the golden ribbons of my heart
that is breaking
into tiny little fragments
sharp enough
to
cut
you
I can't help but wonder what's behind
the venomous touch
that's filled with so much passion
for a heart
that's been squeezed dry
of its golden ribbons that covered
you
all
up.

The Playa's Flava

to all my favorite "playas"

So, what's your flava, playa?

Is she so spicy and red
that you can't get her out of your head
Is she cocoa brown and sweet
where vanilla just can't compete
Is she warm and yellow
melting you to the state of mellow
Is she creamy and caramel
so smooth your passions just yell
Is she bright as amber and honey
making you want to spend all your money
Or, is she toffee, so brown and rich
a taste you just gotta get with...

So playa, what's *your* flava?

Think of Me

Think about me sometimes, huh?...
Remember my smile as you arise to bright sunny days
Remember my affection as the gentle breezes embrace you warmly
Remember my love as the sun shows off beautiful colors in the early sky
Remember my laughter as the flowers beam cheer from their blooms
Remember my passion as cool raindrops dance all over your skin
What ever God enables you to feel or see
Please, just think of me sometimes.

"The Art of Loving Self"

(if the shoe fits...)

Love starts from within
We can't love another, until
We first love ourselves...True? True.

So, because you love yourself so much:
A heart breaks
Because of the thoughtless decisions you make.
Someone's fuse is smoking
Because of a special date unspoken.
Someone has wept through the day and/or night,
Because of loving feelings you constantly fight...
Because you love yourself so much.

Because you love yourself so much:
Someone you claim to care about just doesn't believe you,
Because what you say isn't always what you do.
Hours of sleep were lost waiting on the special occasion of your date,
Because something else, you thought, was more important to make...
Because you love yourself just that much...

Charming...Real Charming.

So, because you are so special to you:
Inconsideration is something you're not aware you do

To a person who genuinely cares for you.
It only takes a minute, out of respect, to change a plan–
Understand that you're only one (woman or) man...
Oh, there are others....

But, see you were the preferred one.
What props do you get for disrespecting someone?
It's humiliating, hurtful, frustrating and exhausting.
I know I'm tired of my time it costing.
Just because "it's" no big deal to you,
Does not mean the feeling is mutual.
But, with you loving you to a greater degree than you should,
That special someone is prevented from seeing just how you actually may be good.

Yes, it's important to first love "you."
It's something we all must do...
But, it's as important to care for and love others–
Something we should have been taught by those who act as our fathers and mothers.

O.K. what I'm saying is this:
You need to change your selfish ways,
'Cause the one you take for granted, you'll surely miss someday.
Sometimes, you must think of someone else

At least as much as you do yourself.
Sometimes, even put that person first...
It will eliminate alot of that hurt
God says, "Love your neighbor, and esteem the other better"
(or, for rhyming reasons, higher)-
It doesn't mean to always deny yourself, but you couldn't be called
selfish or a liar.

Words of endearment can be spoken time and time again,
But, they don't mean a thing if it's not what you're usually showing.
In all seriousness, just do as you say, and say as you'll do,
'Cause, baby, it really, really, really ain't always just about you!

forgotten

when friends were new
there were good times to do
our memories became few
it hurts, but its true...
I was forgotten by you.

GRAND !

written with my cousin, my girl, Sadira McGee
inspired by and dedicated to (the memory of) our cousin, Shaheed Molette...
and to the sisters who have (or have had) broken hearts

Excuse me, but, I don't think you really understand
That, baby, I am GRAND !
Yes, this body would satisfy your urge
But, you need to also absorb the potency of my words
I am not desperate or so insecure that I need to cleave to what's bad
See, I don't think you quite understand, that, baby, I am GRAND !

Cry in my pillow, I think not.
If you choose to leave, then you open the slot
For another chocolate brother,
The perfect sensuous lover...
Why can't you understand,
That replacing you is easy, 'cause, baby, I am GRAND !

You know I'm the type of sistah who'll take care of what I have
But you still have to try me, to have the upper hand
Well, that's ok, do your thing, after all, you are The Man
You think there's more out there for you to seek and make plans...
Sniffing up here and there, thinking you're just The Man
However, you do need to recognize that, baby, I am still GRAND !

I need you in my life... at least that's what you want me to believe
But a sistah of my caliber knows that you're purely a luxury
Item that can be replaced
By the next pretty face
What don't you understand about the fact that
I'm not just a diva...Honey, I'm GRAND!

Playing the games that only a fool could stand
Forgetting the intelligent, articulate, eye-catching woman I am
Please, sugar, come to understand
That I am simply no less than GRAND !

So, what's on <u>your</u> mind?

Use the space below to write your own poem about life and/or love.

I truly appreciate your interest and the time you have taken to read ***a Peace of my Mind...*** I hope you enjoy it. I would love to hear from you and welcome any comments you may have. You may use this form and mail it to Rhythm & Rhyme Publishing, PO Box 444, Antioch, TN 37011-0444. Please, also include (optional) your name, city and state (and e-mail address for a reply). Again, I thank you and look forward to hearing from you.

Order Form

Please process the following order:

Item	Qty *	Subtotal
a Peace of my Mind paperback @ $12.00 ea.		
Shipping & Handling $1.50 per book/ per address	****	
8.25 % Sales Tax (Tennessee residents only)	****	
Total Amount Enclosed	****	

Make check or money order payable to Rhythm & Rhyme Publishing. Mail with order form to Rhythm & Rhyme Publishing, PO Box 444, Antioch, TN 37011-0444. (Photocopy form as needed)

Please ship to:

Name ______________________________

Address ______________________________

City, State, Zip ______________________________

Telephone Number ______________________ (Days)

______________________ (Evenings)

* If ordering books for different "ship to" addresses, please list the additional addresses, and quantity of books for each address, on a separate sheet, and include with this form.